FANTASTIC FIBRE

Written by
John Wood

BookLife
PUBLISHING

©2021
BookLife Publishing Ltd.
King's Lynn
Norfolk PE30 4LS

All rights reserved.
Printed in Malta.

A catalogue record for this book is available from the British Library.

ISBN: 978-1-83927-487-9

Written by:
John Wood

Edited by:
William Anthony

Designed by:
Jasmine Pointer

All facts, statistics, web addresses and URLs in this book were verified as valid and accurate at time of writing. No responsibility for any changes to external websites or references can be accepted by either the author or publisher.

PHOTO CREDITS

All images are courtesy of Shutterstock.com, unless otherwise specified. With thanks to Getty Images, Thinkstock Photo and iStockphoto.

Scientist character throughout – Designbypex. Cover – ShutterStork, Rtstudio, Trong Nguyen, Joshua Resnick, Monkey Business Images. 4–5 – primopiano. 6–7 – Anton Belo, KPG Payless2. 8–9 – Brent Hofacker, Paul Reid, monticello, aleks333. 10–11 – ANURAK PONGPATIMET. 12–13 – Rene Jansa. 14–15 – Paulo Vilela, Surkova. photo. 16–17 – Maks Narodenko, sunabesyou. 18–19 – graletta, sunabesyou. 20–21 – Man-Zu, DronG, DONOT6_STUDIO. 22–23 – Nataliya Arzamasova, LookerStudio, Tim UR, Olha Afanasieva, ifong.

CONTENTS

Page 4   A Slice of Science
Page 6   Portions
Page 8   What Is Fibre?
Page 10 Let's Experiment!
Page 12 Toilet Time
Page 14 Higher Fibre
Page 16 No to Bloat
Page 18 Fibre Insider
Page 20 Food Swaps
Page 23 The Most Important Thing
Page 24 Glossary and Index

Words that look like this can be found in the glossary on page 24.

A SLICE OF SCIENCE

Does everyone keep telling you not to eat too many sweets? Do grown-ups keep putting vegetables on your plate? You might be wondering: why does it matter what I eat?

Hello! I'm a small scientist. I'm here to teach you about food. Food is very important!

You might have heard the words 'healthy diet'. A diet is the kinds of food you usually eat. To have a healthy diet, you need to make sure you eat the right amount of different food.

A healthy diet is often called a balanced diet because you eat lots of different types of food.

PORTIONS

But how do we <u>measure</u> the right amount of food? A portion of food is the right amount you should eat in one sitting.

Sometimes portions are measured in grams. Use a scale like this to find out the right portion size.

A portion of food might be one to four cherry tomatoes.

Different foods have different portion sizes. You should have five portions of fruit and vegetables a day. A portion of fruit is roughly the amount you can fit in the palm of your hand.

WHAT IS FIBRE?

Fibre is found in plant-based food and it is very good for you. Fibre keeps your digestive system healthy. It can also lower your chance of getting heart disease or diabetes later in life.

Look on the next page to see some of the foods that give you lots of fibre.

Bran flakes

LET'S EXPERIMENT!

We will need this mood bar. It will tell us about someone's body. There are four things — how hungry they are, how bloated they feel, how sick and tired they are and how often they go to the toilet.

HUNGER

BLOAT

ENERGY

TOILET

TOILET TIME

She can eat some spinach. Fibre makes people poo more, and also makes poo softer so going to the toilet is easier. Spinach is full of fibre, so this will help our child.

Spinach

Children who are 5 to 11 years old need about 20 grams of fibre a day.

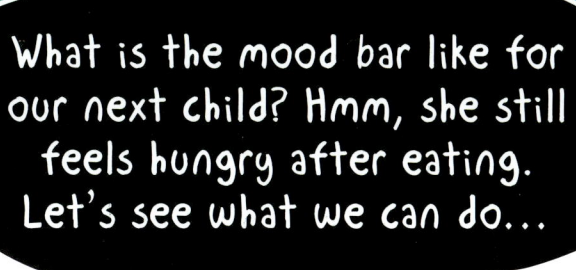

What is the mood bar like for our next child? Hmm, she still feels hungry after eating. Let's see what we can do...

HUNGER

BLOAT

ENERGY

TOILET

HIGHER FIBRE

Feed her <u>wholegrain</u> pasta or brown bread. There is lots of fibre in these foods. If someone still felt hungry after eating, fibre might be a good way to help them.

NO TO BLOAT

Get that child a pear. Feeling bloated is when your stomach feels tight, full and uncomfortable. Fibre can help stop bloating and many fruits, such as pears, have fibre in.

Make sure you eat the skin or peel – that has lots of fibre in it too.

FIBRE INSIDER

Some people can't eat nuts. Turn to page 20 to find out what to eat instead.

Pistachios

What about nuts? Lots of different types of nuts are full of fibre, such as peanuts and pistachios. If you don't get enough fibre, you might get <u>constipated</u> and feel tired.

FOOD SWAPS

Some beans can be a good swap for people with nut allergies. They are full of fibre.

Lima beans

Some people have an <u>allergy</u> to nuts. This can be a very serious and dangerous allergy. It is important that they do not eat nuts or have anything that has a <u>trace</u> of a nut.

Don't worry, there are lots of different foods you can get fibre from. Here are some examples.

Brown rice

Mixed frozen vegetables

Here are even more examples!

Barley porridge

Kidney beans

Carrots

Wholegrain spaghetti

THE MOST IMPORTANT THING

Fibre is very good for you, but don't forget that you must eat lots of different types of food. This is what makes a diet healthy and balanced.

Carbs

Fruit and vegetables

Protein

Fats and sugars

Dairy

GLOSSARY

allergy	when the body reacts to something such as nuts, causing feelings of illness
balanced	made up of the right or equal amounts
constipated	having difficulty pooing
diabetes	a disease in which the body has trouble controlling blood sugar levels, which can lead to damage to organs
digestive system	the parts of the body that work together to break food down and produce energy
heart disease	damage or illness that affects the heart
measure	find out the exact amount of something using units or systems, such as grams for weight or metres for distance
plant-based	something that comes from plants
trace	a very small amount that can hardly be measured
wholegrain	contains the whole of the grain seed and all the nutrients

INDEX

beans 20, 22
bloated 10, 15–16
bread 14
diet 5, 23
fruit 7, 9, 16, 23
grains 8–9, 14, 21–22
hunger 10, 13–14
illness 10, 17
nuts 18, 20
poo 10–12
portions 6–7, 12
rice 21
stomach 16
vegetables 4, 7, 9, 12, 21–23